The Seasons of Pain

by

Kamri Martin

DORRANCE PUBLISHING CO
EST. 1920
PITTSBURGH, PENNSYLVANIA 15238

Dorrance Publishing Co
585 Alpha Drive
Suite 103
Pittsburgh, PA 15238
Visit our website at *www.dorrancebookstore.com*

ISBN: 979-8-89027-214-0
eISBN: 979-8-89027-712-1

To those who have impacted who I am.
To those who have impacted who I want to be.

Read this when you are lost.

I am ready to be heard.

Everyone has a voice, but it is up to you to use it.
It doesn't matter how I tell the story, how you perceive it is how you will see me, it's how I tell it to myself.

I felt like roadkill that was constantly being run over.
I didn't want a knight in armor, but I didn't want to save myself.
I was a community service worker picking up everyone's problems as if they were my responsibility and carrying them over my shoulder along with my own.
It was weighing me down and wearing me out.
I was drenched with peoples' issues and rung dry of advice.
I was exhausted.
I felt as if I were holding everyone up while everyone was letting me down.
At some point, you have to take a step back and evaluate what's happening and who you are growing away from. Or pushing away from. We know companionship is what keeps us afloat and yet we tend to sink ourselves and others.
I was hurt, over and over, like most people.

But an extremely wise man once told me, being in the gutter means you're alive.

WINTER

SPRING

SUMMER

Winter

The darkness is harsh in the blizzard of depression I was flung into as
the cold reality piled up against my chest hearing you get into the car
and drive away for the last time.
Numb and aching as I try to recover from the frostbite I got when
you left me.
Trying to warm up without further damaging my wounds.
Trying to thaw who I was before you came along.

Why We Could Never Be

The story of us was not what it seemed.

You're the sun and I'm the sea, getting close enough to kiss until you leave.

Fire and gasoline, you hurt me when I was trying to help you grow.

I accepted you and you rejected me.

I was careful with everything I did and said, you were careless and broke my heart.

I run to you and you run from me.

We clash and I compromise to your needs.

Black and white.
Silver and gold.
The sun and the moon.
Love and hate.
You and me.

I drown in my sorrows, crying tsunamis and hurricanes.

You look at them like they are a mist that won't flood your sailboat.

You set your mind to an ocean with more fish.

I cast out my dreams and was vulnerable waiting for you to bite the

bait so I could bring you back to me.

You drew all the wishes from my well and shattered them one by one.

You ripped my heart out and watched me bleed out with no sorrow.

You held me up and I hit the ground harder.

All I did was give.

All you did was take.

I poured into you, emptying myself of everything I was.

I gave time. I gave energy. I gave encouragement.

I poured and poured until I was empty.

Then I refilled and did it again and again.

I put my wellbeing aside for you.

I thought we were unstoppable but you pulled the emergency break.

Now I'm the moon.
Hiding in the darkness.
Hiding my sadness.
Hiding my hurt.
Hiding my heart.
Hiding pieces of me from anyone that tried to get close.

Some people never have to shine alone in the darkness.
Hoping for change, hoping to get a chance, hoping something changes.

I'm the moon.
And you're a morning person.

You refuse to acknowledge my darkness because that would make
your world dark.

You feel more alone in the dark.
Your demons come back at night.
You get a glimpse of how the moon feels.
You feel the pain I am living in.

I was selfless and you were selfish.
You decided you were more important and entitled than I could ever become.
When I was down in the dumps, I let you toss your trash on me.

I wanted what was going to make you happy and whole no matter how broken it was going to make me.

You made me a sliver of what I could've become and convinced me it was all I'd ever be.
You made me feel incompetent and insignificant.

If you get too close to the sun, you get burnt.
That's why some nights it's not a full moon.

I chipped away pieces of myself to change for you and I can't get them back.

My burns are still visible.
My heart still aches.
I'm still recovering.

I'm winter and you're summer.

I became spring and it poured.

You, the sun, were there to show hope only after the sky was done crying.
Maybe the sky loved the ground and felt bad for burning it, so it cried
to wash away the heat.
Maybe the sky cried because it saw the sun and moon and didn't
understand why they weren't together.

You thought the rain was useless.
You wanted to be in a desert when my tears poured out for you.
You craved hate when I loved.
You craved lies when I told the truth.
You craved space when I gave you attention.

The sun needed no one.
Shining alone was your nature.

I started to realize you would always be fall.

You would always be changing leaves.

You would always be blown to another location.

You would always be one foot out the door.

You came from a tree that's environment was constantly altering.

You were prepared to run and hide.

Prepared to leave the side of people who care, who you were never there for.

Prepared to flee the crime scene you left in others.

Leaving was in your roots even when you swore you would change.

You follow in the footsteps that your father placed in front of you.

Your apple did not leave the side of the tree you came from.

Commitment issues.

You have never allowed yourself to love anyone.
You have never allowed yourself to care for anyone.
You have never allowed yourself to feel the pain of losing someone.
No one ever taught you and you never took it upon yourself to learn.
You can't forgive yourself, you don't think anyone else can.

You can't see yourself how others see you, so you destroy their image.
What a foolish way of life, simply because you're incapable of
something doesn't mean the whole world has your weakness.

When you are blind, there are thousands of others who can see what
you can't.

When you are in the dark, there are thousands in the light.

Your weaknesses are someone's strengths.

What I wanted and what you wanted were polar opposites.

We were on separate sides of the universe trying to understand each other.

There would have always been something in the way.

I never asked for this.
I never asked to be lied to.
I never asked to be betrayed.
I never asked to be dark.
I never asked for the pain or demons.

You made me the moon and then you made me hate the moon.

To me, it was too dark, too quiet, too much to handle.
Although it isn't as much responsibility as the sun, people look up to
the moon.
A symbol of hope at night when the darkness is surrounding their hearts.

I can't be that for them.
I can't be anything they want me to be.
I am broken and I can't be put on display for all to see.
I can't have people expecting things from me that I can't give.
I can't be someone's hope when I am looking for my own.
I can't be someone's guide when I am lost.

Maybe it was never love. Maybe it never could've been.
Love is so simple, yet we make it the hardest thing ever and then it is
not love.

We alter our definition of love to equal our expectations and when we
don't get what we want we declare that people don't love us.

They are going to do what they want to anyway, at the end of the day,
we all do.

We are victims of our own robbery of joy.
We stop ourselves from being happy as often as traffic lights change in
a big city.

Our happiness is up to us.

We go into denial thinking bad things won't happen to us.

Maybe because we have had too much bad and think it counts for our

lifetime.

We let ourselves down.

We raise our expectations for the world.

We want someone else to be responsible.

Someone to be in charge of the happiness and take care of the sadness.

We try to give it to someone else to handle because we have done a

poor job of doing it ourselves.

We get in the way of ourselves.

We hold ourselves back.

We hold each other back.

We get caught up on what could have been, not thinking about how it could've possibly been worse than what was going on.
We get stuck on how we believe things should've turned out.

We distract ourselves and it makes everything worse once we remember what has happened, and sometimes what hasn't happened.

We forget we hold our future, our happiness, our lives in our own hands.
We forget we own our own world.

There is nothing you could say to make up for the bruising and scarring.

Even if there was, it is not like you would come back to say it.

You wouldn't have let us be together if I moved mountains for you.

After all this time, I have finally accepted that we would never be together because you never wanted to be with me.

Spring

I am trying to rebloom, regrow, and retrust my feelings.

Things I wish someone would've told me

I push myself into a tiny box and keep everyone else as the fully
focused picture.

I take better care of others than I do myself.

I put people up on a pedestal, even though it will end with me feeling
intensely unappreciated.

I plan for the worst of things to happen because I need to be prepared
instead of blindsided.

I'm overly apologetic because receiving apologies in my life was rare.

I blame myself for anything and everything that goes wrong because
I was always the one taking responsibility.

No matter whose actions they were, I was the one who cleaned up the mess.

I hold people close or push them far because my life has been
overwhelmingly full of inconsistency; extremities are all I ever learned.

Things I wish someone would've told me.

Let me in on the secret of me.

I wish people were honest instead of hiding how they felt.

I wish everyone knew how it felt to be taking care of everyone else
when it feels like no one will take care of you when you need it.

Why did we promise things to break them?

When did we become a burden not a blessing?

How did they not feel bad about the way they left things?

How did you not look back and check to make sure I was breathing?

Signs of who you are are stapled to me.

I hear your thoughts in my head.
I hear your words when I talk.
I hear your laugh within my own.

I see your habits within mine.

It all begins somewhere.
Every ending is the start of something else.

Your smirk began to sting.
Your laugh began to sound evil.
Your hands began to shake.
Your eyes began to display betrayal.
Your feelings began to fade.
You began to leave.

I began to plead.
I began to bargain.
I began to cry.
I began to scream.
I began to understand.
I began to release you.

I couldn't fight for you or for myself anymore.

It all seemed pointless and tiring.

It hurt more to hold onto thorns than it would to let go of the flower.

I never knew someone could hurt me by using the way I loved them.

I had to preserve the leftover pieces of myself.

I didn't want you to know that you had an immense impact on me.

That you changed the way I talk, the way I laugh, the way I think.

That you changed the way I see others.

That you changed the way I communicate.

That you helped shape me into someone I had been trying to be for years.

Now you're gone.

And so is who I used to be.

Seasons come and go and you venture with them.

There was always a piece of me that felt horrible about the things you did and the way you handled them.

I wanted to believe you were being truthful.

I hoped there was a tiny part of you that was still who I thought I knew.

I hoped there was still good in you.

I hoped you could change like you promised.

I hoped you could remember the good times and stop creating the bad.

I hoped it was a bad nightmare that I could wake up from.

Sadly, it was a nightmare I woke up in, with tears stained on my cheek.

You broke my heart into microscopic pieces that a broom couldn't pick up.

You held me down and clips my wings, while I stood there thinking it was out of love.

I was trying to save you when I'm the one who needed to be saved.

You kept restating that it wasn't my fault that I am broken. Great, because every crying girl wants to hear that even her knight in shining armor decided that the dragons were too difficult to handle. That the demons were too tough to fight, and it was easier to surrender and turn around leaving her in the dust.

You left and it changed me entirely.
I took off my crown and embraced my horns.
I felt the ice settle behind my rib cage.
I felt the fire burning in my veins.
I looked into the mirror at a stranger.
I had settled into what I believed my fate was.

You told me that people always leave and it's a sad fact of life.

I figured out that people leave because it's what we are used to.
She left you.
You left me.

It's a torturous cycle and everyone's epilogue reads hurt.

People leave and if you force them to stay they become unhappy.

People leave for various reasons.
Some people leave because they are incapable of loving anyone but
themselves.
Some people leave because it's all they have ever known.
Some people leave because they think it's in your best interest but
really it's because they know they will hurt you again.
Some people leave because they are scared.
Some people leave because you remind them of someone who hurt them.
Some people leave because they can't handle any more pain.
Some people leave because it's easier to say goodbye than it is to tell
their feelings.
Some people leave because they can't keep watching themselves hurt you.
Some people leave because they are empty and don't want to hollow
you out.

You never showed anyone your dull moments, except me.

You were scared that they would run from the monster instead of hugging it.

No one understood you like I did, nor would they be able to and that scared you.

I was your sidekick, I took care of you when you wouldn't take care of yourself.

You won't let them break away pieces of your turtle shell opening you up to the pain.

All the girls will never be able to fill the empty space in you.

Not even all the alcohol.

Alcohol will damage your liver and make you more sad.

You feel alone wishing no one would have let you leave.

We had to let go.

It hurt to stay and be pushed back and forth from meaning something
to nothing to you.

There was no sign of hope for you coming back and staying.

We got tired of waiting for you to accept us and be proud of us.

We needed something sturdy, something to help hold us together from
the last time you broke us.

If an ocean were between us you were supposed to be willing to meet
me halfway.

I wish I had the chance to tell you some things before you went with the wind.

You shouldn't have to go through life alone.
You shouldn't stop yourself from getting things you want because you don't believe they will last.

I used to wish at every 11:11 that you would get better than you deserve, wishing that you wouldn't settle for less.
You deserve to know what it's like to be truly happy.
I was rooting for you.
Thank you for all the things you ever did for me.
Even when I got hurt, I learned.
You taught me how to be there for myself.
You taught me to stand up for my feelings.
You taught me how to build boundaries.

People deserve more chances than you were ever willing to give.

I guess it's harder to ignore your problems when they come knocking at your doorstep, begging to be acknowledged.

You shoved us into the box of dead roses and stored us into your attic of lost feelings with no intention of returning.

Slicing our hearts until they were nothing because we meant nothing to you.

Summer

Finally feeling the sun on my face again. Appreciating the other seasons but enjoying the fresh air.

To heal you have to accept your past.

How to breathe again

Nothing hurts quite as bad as betrayal.

Over time, no matter what anyone says, the pain gets easier to handle.

It's not right away and some days you will break down.
It's never the end of the world, no matter how bad it feels.
It's like having phantom limb syndrome, it hurts and hurts but at
some point, you get used to them being gone.

One day you wake up and it isn't the first thing you think about.
One day you will walk past a place that used to dig in your heart and
it won't make you cry.
One day you will hear their name and it won't make you wince.
One day you will realize you had to lose them to gain yourself.

It gets worse and then better.
The worst will be the worst it's ever been.
But it's worth the cons.

You will be okay again.

I know it's scary to think of life without them.
No matter who it was or what happened, it is always scary.

You don't know what you'd do or who you'd be without them.
You don't know who you can tell important things anymore.
You have never had to picture it until now and it's hurtful and makes
you fearful.
You start to close yourself off because your trust has been
compromised by someone you thought would never do this to you.
We lose people and go through our own grief patterns.
You grow from the pain of the things you've gone through.

It's the feeling that washes over you in waves but hollows you out at
the same time.

Here are some steps to help

Forgive all those who have done you wrong. At first it will feel like betrayal towards yourself. In the end, you'll carry less burdens. Your heart will thank you in time.

Delete pictures. No matter if you cry the whole time.

Delete text messages. You won't forget what they said but it will help that you can't look at them.

Stop eating ice cream every night. It will, without fail, remind you that you're sad.

Walk new paths without him by your side.

Listen to new music.

Love yourself even if he couldn't.

Encourage yourself even though he wouldn't.

Go on a walk.

Better yourself.

Talk to someone about what is going on.

Give closure to yourself.

Take some time to be by yourself, to breathe and recover.

Whatever you're feeling is normal.

It is perfectly normal to feel angry and even unintelligent.
It is normal to feel let down by yourself because you didn't see this coming.
It is normal to sulk.
It is normal to not want to move forward with life for a little.
It is normal to feel loss.
It is normal to reminisce on the good time that you had and be upset that they are gone.
It is normal to see the person that hurt you and have to focus on breathing because it hurts to see them.
Your life randomly changed right before your eyes and it wasn't what you were expecting.
It is normal to feel hurt and surprised and to not be okay.
Don't let anyone try to control your emotions.

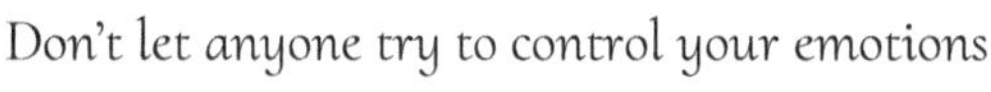

You must conquer your sadness before you will conquer your circumstances.

Don't let anyone put a timer on your healing process for it is yours.

However you feel, is acceptable.
However you heal, is acceptable.

You're getting up from a far fall.
You need time to be completely healed.
You can't push the hurt out and act like it's not there or it will get worse.
You do not have to fix yourself right after you are broken.
You can't heal unless you are ready for it.

Sometimes you have to be your own knight in shining armor.

You have to save yourself from the abuse.
You have to slay your own dragons.
You have to rescue yourself.
You have to be there for yourself.
You have to hold yourself together.
You have to rely on yourself.
You have to force yourself to do the things that help you heal even
when they hurt.

Let them be a memory.

Going over the memories countless times is not going to make them hurt less.
Ignoring the memories isn't going to make you forget everything that happened.
Let those memories rest in peace.

If by some miracle they walk back into your life, and you can't tell them no, do not get comfortable.
They left.
No matter how hard you try, you'll never be as close as you were.
You'll never feel completely comfortable around them.

They made a monster out of you.
You needed them and they walked away.
And it is probable that it will happen again.

They are sorry, I get it. I've heard it.
Being sorry does not erase all the tears you cried.
It doesn't take back all the horrible things they said.
It doesn't tape up the hole in your heart.
It won't conclude all the pain you feel.

Everyone has limits and boundaries.

There's only so much hurt and strain your heart can take before it
begs not to feel anything.

You had a line and they crossed it.

They used their power in your life.

They stretched your patience, trust, and love thin.

They got you to change rules you never thought you would change.

They made you believe everything they said was true.

Then they left, like you meant nothing to them.

Now it's truly best for everyone if they stay on the other side of the line.

Distance makes the healing process more effective.
It helps when you don't have to constantly deal with the person that
is causing you hurt.
Moths are still attracted to the light knowing it burns, we are the same.
We know they hurt us but they have become our familiarity so we try
running back to see if anything has changed.
It hasn't and it won't.
You can't keep going back to the people who hurt you expecting them
to care for you.
They will always have a piece of you, you don't automatically get it back.
You have to learn to adapt to missing some parts of you.
It is unfair and frustrating, but it is the process.

You can't want a person to change without letting them know what
they did wrong.
Standing in the openness of their mistakes will make them angry and
lash out.
They take it out on you when they can't take it out on themselves.

If they are inconsistent with words and actions, they are not worth
the pain they're putting you through.

You don't need them.
You only need yourself.
No one values your dreams and success like you.

One day you'll believe it.
You are enough.

You have to learn when to walk away when only hurt and heartbreak
are being served in your relationship.
You have to learn when to walk away when there is nothing good left.

We hold on to the good moments for too long hoping there will be
another one, and when there isn't, we still have hope from the last one
and we are continuously waiting.

Being pulled by an emotional string does not have to be your forte.

You should never have to beg someone to treat you like a human being.
You should never have to beg someone to care about you as much as
you care about them.
You should never have to beg someone to stay in your life.

It's not love if they make you hate yourself.

It's not love if they make you change everything that makes you you.

It's not love if they beat you down and break you.

It's not love if they make you question your worth.

You shouldn't have to run after people to prove you matter.

You matter.

If someone can't see it, then it is not your responsibility to try to prove it to them.

You do not owe anyone anything.

If they can't see the good about you, the only thing that matters is that you can still see it.

Love is a choice.

You choose to look past the mistakes and imperfections because you would rather have them instead of lose them.

You choose to let people walk over you because you love them enough to realize they need someone there to remain standing.

You choose to wake up in the morning and talk to the people you do because you care about them.

You choose to stay and put up with the bad days because you can't imagine the good days with anyone else.

You choose to take care of this person better than they take care of themselves.

You choose to let this person in and let them know every quirk about you hoping that your love is enough for them to stay through the bad times.

Love is an action.

It is showing people you care about them more than yourself.

It is proving yourself to someone time and time again when they think you will let them down.

It is pushing away things that would make your person feel unappreciated or insecure.

It is continuously giving your all, whether it is 100% that day or 40%.

They stole your light.

They took everything that you had in you.

They damaged your heart and darkened your soul.

You're darker than ever and you don't see a way out of the darkness.

It's hard to see the good when you're surrounded by the bad.

I know that it feels like the world is on top of you, smashing you to pieces.

I know you want to crawl into a ball and disappear.

You want to forget everything and nothing at once.

You want to keep the good memories but they carve into your heart every time they come around.

You want to feel something other than hurt.

You want to be told everything is going to be okay.

You want to wake up and be whole and healed.

Even if it's everything you've ever feared, even if it's the hardest thing
you do, you will live without them.

You will grow from this.
You will be able to breathe again.
You will be okay again.
You will be whole again.
You will smile again.
You will laugh again.

One day their name won't sting like a thousand bees.
One day their arms won't be what you consider home.
One day you'll be stronger and braver.

Take deep breaths.
The pain will slowly fade away.

Don't forget how you felt or how long you felt it.
Someone in your life will need help going through something similar
and you need to show them that you can survive it.

You're not alone on this sinking ship.

You are never alone, no matter how lonely you feel.

Someone else is feeling the same way you are.

Pain is universal.

There are people feeling every single feeling you are.

We understand you, even when you can't understand yourself.

You are a survivor.

You survived their strong winds and nasty storms.
You survived your pool of tears.
You survived the nights where you were so gone you couldn't walk.

No turning back, you have made it this far.

I believe in you even if no one else does.
Even when you don't.

I thought I was like Humpty, never to be whole again, but I was wrong.

I broke the spell and I was set free.

It became clear, all the bullshit I had just been through was not my fault.

There was nothing I could've done to change the way they treated me.

If I can rise from the ashes of myself after they continuously burned me, then you can too.

You will rise above them and prove to them that you would've given them the world but they could not do anything to deserve it.

You are nothing bad that they have made you feel.
You are none of the labels they slapped onto you when they were angry.
You are not what they say.

Don't let someone who couldn't be fully truthful about their feelings make you feel like you are less than deserving of all the good things the world has to offer.

Do not let them define you.

Do not let the old you, the angry you, the hurt you, define you.

You are you.

You are important.

You are strong.

You are smart.

You are kind.

You bring sunlight to the darkness.

You are worth everything.

You are more than gold.

You are the salt of the earth.

The stars spell your name.

Do not chase butterflies just to find yourself being stung by bees.
Do not stoop to their level because you could find yourself unable to
get up.
Do not cry anymore because they are not crying for you.
Do not beat yourself up for something you couldn't control.
Do not stay stuck in a state of mind where you're drowning.

Grab your oars, whether it be friends, family or chocolate, and row
the hell away from them.
Row away from the negative feelings.
Row away from the memories.
Row away from the place where they left you.
Row to people who care for you.

People who care about you don't want to watch you bleed.
Your support team doesn't want to watch you fail.

If they cared for you, they wouldn't have strung you along by the strings of your heart.
They would've been protecting you.
They would've been honest and careful.

They gave you up.
You don't deserve to suffer in pain.

Do not belittle yourself even though they did.
Do not start believing all the negative things they said about you.

Maybe you had to let them go.
It was your survival instincts, you had to protect your heart from the same hurt it had been enduring.
When their patterns are so predictable you have to let go before they do to save yourself.
You had to walk away while you could.
You knew how it was going to end, why give them the power when you already know what is going to happen.
You did the right thing, no matter how much it hurts.
You didn't lose them, they lost you.

If you keep running back to what hurt you, you will never fully be okay.

Sometimes you don't get to say goodbye.

Some people can't handle it.

Some people can't say bye, they've never had people in their life who have stayed so they keep their distance and are cautious not to get attached.

Some people wake up one morning and decide it is time to end things now so they won't get hurt later.

They can't handle the closing remarks of what your friendship or relationship was to them.

They can't reminisce about the times they had with you, knowing there will be no more.

They can't give you a proper statement to close up all your questions about what happened or how they feel about it.

They can't let your hand touch their face one last time.

They can't handle thinking about what the future is going to be without you.

If they do, they won't want to leave and it will be harder for them to ignore their sadness.

So they don't say goodbye.

It would hurt them too much and they can't bring themselves to look at you and thank you for everything you have done.
It would hurt you too much to hear all the memories that were their favorite knowing they are leaving.
It would hurt you to listen to them go on and on about why they have to leave.
It would hurt them too much when you fight for them to stay.

Maybe it is you who can't handle the goodbyes.

Fight the urge to run before handing out closure.

Fight the urge to distance yourself before they get too close to you.

Fight the urge to not let anyone in.

You have been hurt before, not everyone will leave.

Not everyone will lie.

Not everyone will betray you.

You have to keep letting people in to find the good ones.

The ones that stay.

The ones that are brutally honest because they know all the lies you have ever been told.

The ones that support you.

The ones that would follow you into war even if all you had to fight with was a spoon.

Find your people.

And hold on to them.

One day you'll find closure, whether it's a made up story about what
happened or the actual story, but you can't keep sitting around
waiting for it. You have to learn how to live without it.

When people don't say bye you have to learn to say it yourself.
You know how it feels to not receive it, so give it.
Say goodbye, thank people for their spot in your story.
Say thank you.
Say I will miss you.
And if they don't say it back, it doesn't mean they don't feel it.
They can't let themselves believe that goodbye is real.

It may seem impossible to recover and let people in now but be still,
and do not lose heart.

It is okay to be scared about the future.

At first, I was scared.

I was scared to move on.

I was scared that I'd be wasting time.

I was scared that I would never be enough.

I was broken so many times that I started to expect it.

I was scared that no one could reciprocate my feelings.

I was terrified that I would turn into everyone that hurt me.

If you're not careful you will.

You'll start being the monster that you've dealt with all of your life.

You'll be the one pushing people away.

You'll be the one starting fights.

You'll be the one ruining the best thing that's happened to you.

You won't notice the signs at first.

History only repeats itself if you let it.

Stop allowing your past to spoil your future.

Do not burn the bridge that is keeping you from drowning.

Do not become who you've been running from.

Remember the cycle.

Break the cycle.

You don't have to keep doing everything you have ever known.
You don't have to become the person who broke you.
Change is not always the worst thing in the world.

Pick up the pieces of yourself and go find the nearest table.
You have to put yourself together.
You have to be the glue.
You have to take care of yourself.
You have to love yourself.
You have to stop blaming yourself for what happened.

Beating yourself up doesn't take away any pain.

You will flourish when you begin watering yourself.

You will sprout and bloom.

You will grow into a better version of the person you were.

You will attract better people, safer people.

You have to be willing to continue working on yourself.

You will not see overnight results.

It takes a while and it hurts.

Sometimes you have to relearn all the things that you forgot during the pain.

You have to teach yourself things that seem so simple but get lost in the process of grieving.

You have to relearn to see yourself in a positive way.

To stop worrying so much.

To stop disconnecting from those who care.

To let your heart heal.

To keep a reasonable distance from those who hurt you.

To let go.

Faking it doesn't fix it.

It just prolongs the process of it being fixed.

Anger does not fix it.

You can't build an empire off of anger.

You need sturdy.

You need unbreakable.

You need to believe in yourself and be the cause you're building for.

You need to put down other peoples' baggage while building.

You can't stand in quicksand with everyone's problems on your

shoulder or you will sink faster.

You can't always take responsibility for other people.

Let them grow up while you grow into who you can be.

You can only take so much before you wear down.

The weary that wears out the heart wears out the body.

Don't let the demons in your head take over your life.
You are the light, even when you feel dark.

You have to give yourself the things you deserve before you can allow
someone else to do it.

You deserve your name written in the stars.
You deserve endless love notes.
You deserve to be cared for.
You deserve to be treated with respect.
You deserve the world and more.
You deserve more than you could imagine.

Do not let someone else make you feel undeserving.
You hold your worth in your hands.

Do not settle for less.

You will love again.

There's no darkness too dark for love to be in.

During the wait it is painful and difficult to keep hope but once you find it, it is worth all the suffering you had to endure.

You can do it.

Acknowledgements

It was hard to feel these feelings all over again. To see what I had actually put myself through and called it love. Thank you to my wonderful sister for always reading what I have to say and supporting me. Thank you, Somer, for always answering my questions and being very patient with me. Thank you, Steven Dunn, for reminding me that even in the gutter, I was alive. Thank you, Kristopher, although you had no part in my past, you love me for who I am now and think all my glued puzzle pieces are a masterpiece. I love you. Thank you to Katy Antimarino, Taryn Wells, Rachael Bindas, and the Dorrance Publishing team, with your support, expertise, and confidence I have the comfortability to work with you to publish my book. Thank you to those who hurt me. You have shown me who I don't want to be. You showed me how to understand the change I can't control. This isn't about one person; I took in account all the heartbreaks and all the life altering things that had happened to me. I want to thank everyone for reading this; you make it possible for me to use my voice and spread my story.

9 7 9 8 8 8 9 0 2 7 2 1 4 0